Let's Explore!

HOW THINGS WORK

ARCTURUS

ARCTURUS

This edition published in 2021 by Arcturus Publishing Limited
26/27 Bickels Yard, 151–153 Bermondsey Street,
London SE1 3HA

Author: Polly Cheeseman
Illustrator: Jean Claude
Editor: Violet Peto
Designer: Stefan Holliland
Consultant: Anne Rooney
Managing Editor: Joe Harris

ISBN: 978-1-83940-835-9
CH008328NT
Supplier 29, Date 0721, Print run 10750

Printed in China

CONTENTS

WHAT MAKES BICYCLES GO?

Bicycles are machines that help us get from one place to another.

The handlebars change the direction of the front wheel.

To stop the bicycle, you squeeze the brakes, and little pads push against the wheels to stop the bicycle.

The pedals are connected to a gear. The back wheel has a gear, too. Both gears are linked by a chain.

When you turn the pedals, it drags the chain around which turns the back wheel.

When the back wheel turns, it pushes the bicycle forward and forces the front wheel to turn.

HOW DO SHOES STAY FASTENED?

There are simple but clever inventions we use to fasten our shoes.

Some shoes use laces, others use buckles, and some use hook-and-loop fasteners.

Hook-and-loop fasteners are made of strips of material that stick together.
They are also used on clothes, shoes, bags, and other household things. Can you spot any in your home?
One side is covered with soft loops.
The other side has strong strands with tiny hooks on the ends.
When the two sides are pressed together, the hooks grip onto the loops.

HOW DO DISHWASHERS CLEAN DISHES?

Dishwashers are machines that clean and rinse your dirty dishes.

The dishwasher was invented more than 130 years ago. The first dishwasher worked in a similar way to the ones we use today!

A pump heats up water and pushes it into the spray arms.

The spray arms turn around, spraying clean water onto the dishes.

Dishwashers need electricity and water to work.

A soap compartment pops open during the wash. The soap mixes with the water in the machine.

HOW DOES A SPACECRAFT LAUNCH?

Launch vehicles are used to send spacecraft and satellites into space. They need rocket power to get there.

Rockets help blast the launch vehicle into space. They burn fuel until it runs out. The empty rockets drop back to Earth. Some can be collected and used again.

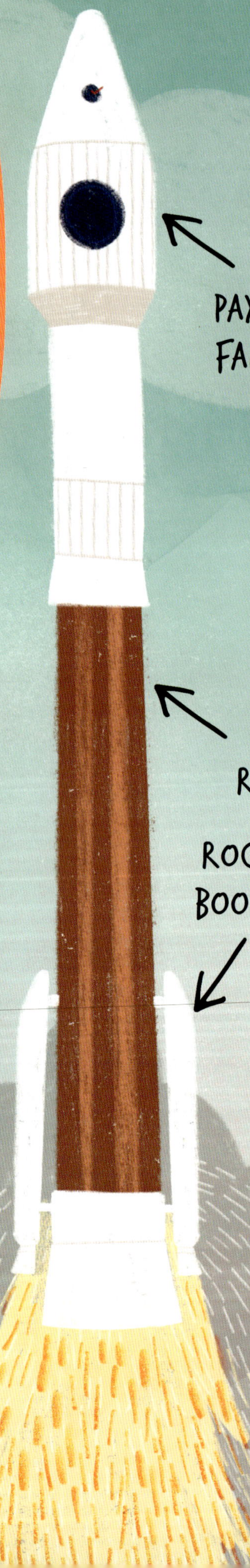

The spacecraft is contained inside a nose cone called the payload fairing.

The fuel in the rockets needs oxygen to burn. We normally find oxygen as a gas in the air.

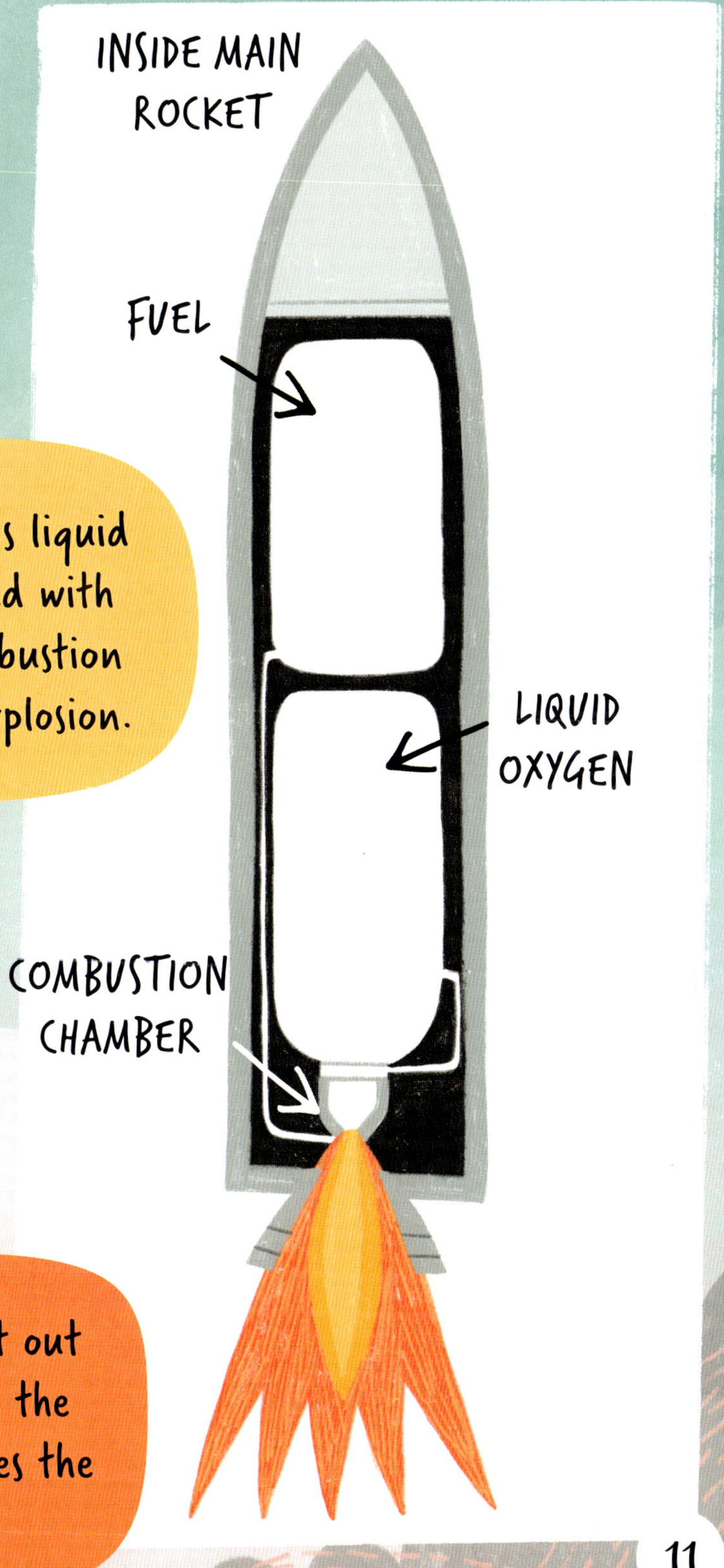

Inside the rocket, there is liquid oxygen. When it is mixed with fuel in the rocket's combustion chamber, it makes an explosion.

Waste gases blast out and down from the rocket. This forces the rocket up.

WHAT KEEPS A LOCK LOCKED?

We keep our homes safe by locking the doors.

When you turn the key in a lock, a piece of metal goes in and out. This is called the deadbolt.

The key has parts cut out of it in a special pattern.

Inside the lock there is a set of levers, which let the deadbolt move in and out.

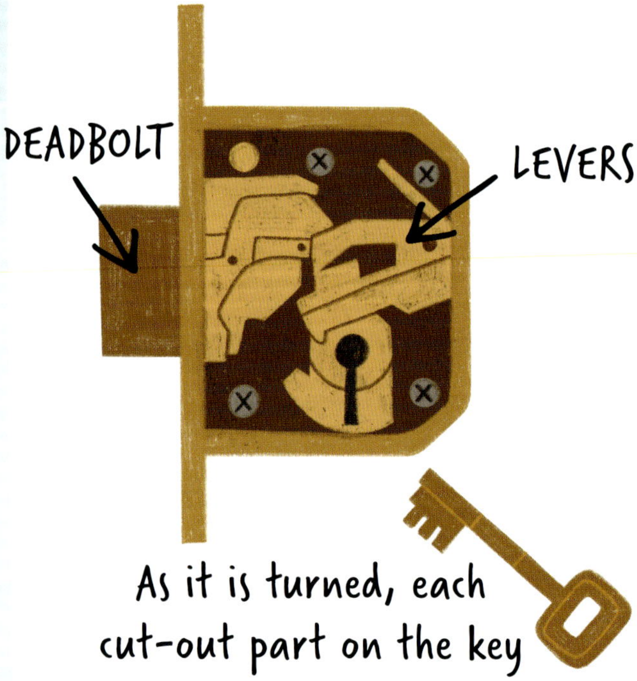

As it is turned, each cut-out part on the key lines up with a lever.

When all the levers line up, the deadbolt slides back into the lock.

When the deadbolt is inside the lock, the door can open. When the deadbolt slides into the slot in the door frame, it holds the door in place.

HOW DOES A PHONE MAKE A CALL?

Cellular phones are a handy way to keep in touch with friends and family.

When you talk, a tiny microphone inside the phone picks up your voice and turns the sounds into an electrical signal.

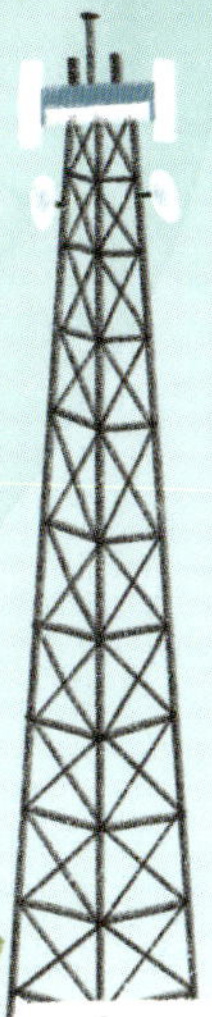

The phone turns the signal into radio waves. Radio waves are invisible waves of energy that can travel through the air and space.

A tall structure at a base station receives the radio waves.

The base station sends the radio waves to a central station in the area.

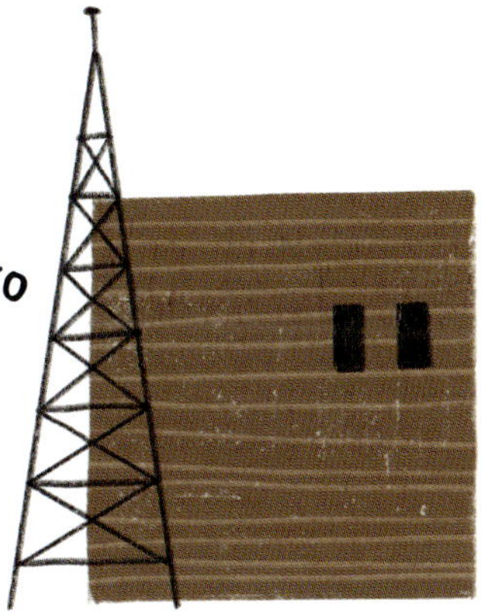

The central station sends the radio waves to a base station close to your friend.

That base station sends the radio waves to their phone.

Their phone receives the radio waves and changes them back into sounds.

HOW DOES A VACUUM CLEANER WORK?

A vacuum cleaner sucks up dust and dirt from your floor.

When you turn the vacuum cleaner on, the motor makes a fan spin very fast.

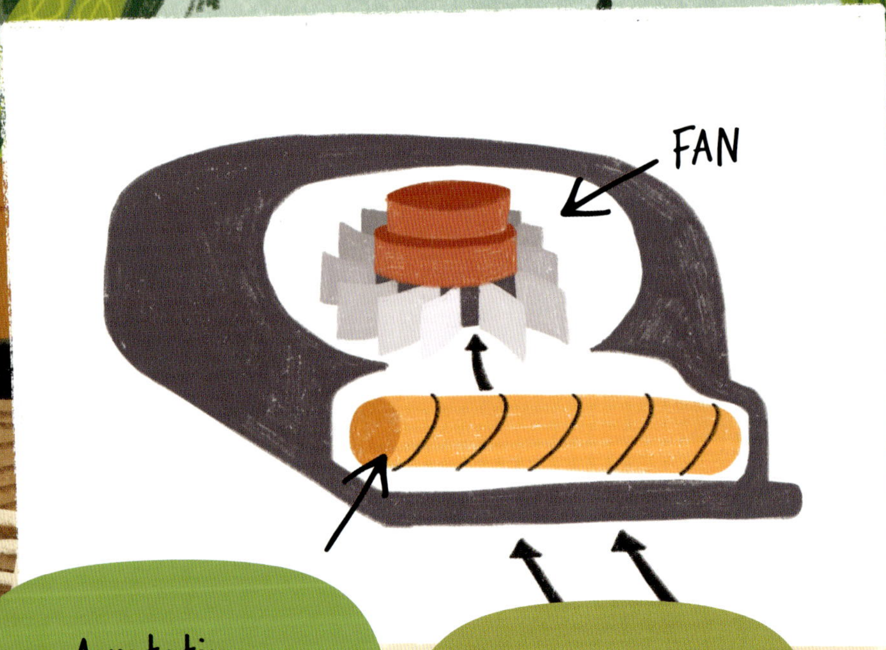

A rotating (spinning) brush at the front loosens all the dust and dirt from the floor.

The fan spins so quickly that it sucks in air, dust, and dirt.

The filter traps small particles of dust while larger particles spin around inside the container.

Clean air flows out.

Dirty air is sucked up by the fan through a pipe and into the container.

When the container is full of dust and dirt, it is emptied, ready for next time.

Some vacuum cleaners have bags that the dirt goes into, and some have see-through containers. But they all work in the same way!

HOW DOES A PILOT STEER A HELICOPTER?

Helicopters can move up, down, forward, backward, and sideways! They can even hover or stay in one place in the air.

Helicopters are very useful in an emergency, because they can fly almost anywhere.

The engine turns the rotor blades really fast to lift the helicopter into the air.

A smaller tail rotor keeps the helicopter from spinning around in circles.

The main rotor blades are connected to the swash plate. The pilot tilts the swash plate, which makes the rotors tilt.

When the rotors tilt forward, the helicopter moves forward. When they tilt back, the helicopter moves backward.

Each rotor blade is shaped so that the air flows over the top of it quickly.

HOW DO PENS MAKE MARKS?

Hundreds of years ago, people wrote and drew pictures using the tip of a feather dipped in ink. It was very messy!

Ballpoint pens were invented in the 1930s.

A ballpoint pen has a thin plastic tube inside. The tube is filled with quick-drying ink.

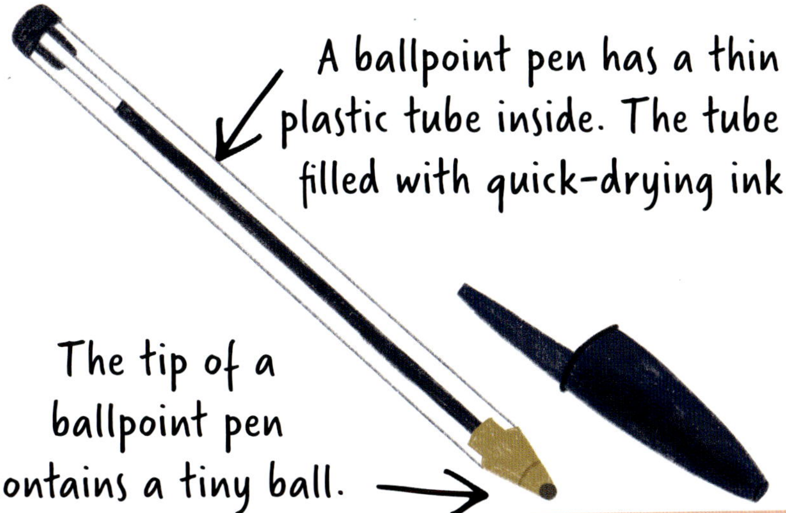

The tip of a ballpoint pen contains a tiny ball.

As you push the pen across paper, the ball rolls around and gets coated with ink. The pen leaves a line of ink on the paper.

The nib (tip) of a felt-tip pen is made from nylon. The nib soaks up ink from the main part of the pen.

HOW DOES A COMPUTER WORK?

A computer, such as a laptop or tablet, is a machine that follows a set of instructions. It makes calculations and stores information.

The parts of a computer you can touch are called hardware.

Information goes into the computer through the keyboard, mouse, camera, or touchscreen.

A program is a set of instructions a computer follows to complete a task. Together, programs are called software.
This is the screen. Screens, printers, and speakers are called output devices.
Inside the computer, a device called a processor receives the information and decides what to do next.
The processor works like a brain. It deals with all the information that goes into and out of the computer. It is small but very powerful.

HOW DOES AN ONLINE GAME WORK?

Online games send messages through the Internet. The Internet is a system that connects millions of computers around the world.

The Internet lets computers "talk" to each other. Information, such as words, pictures, and videos can be sent from one computer to another.

Online games use the Internet to connect players so they can share their moves.

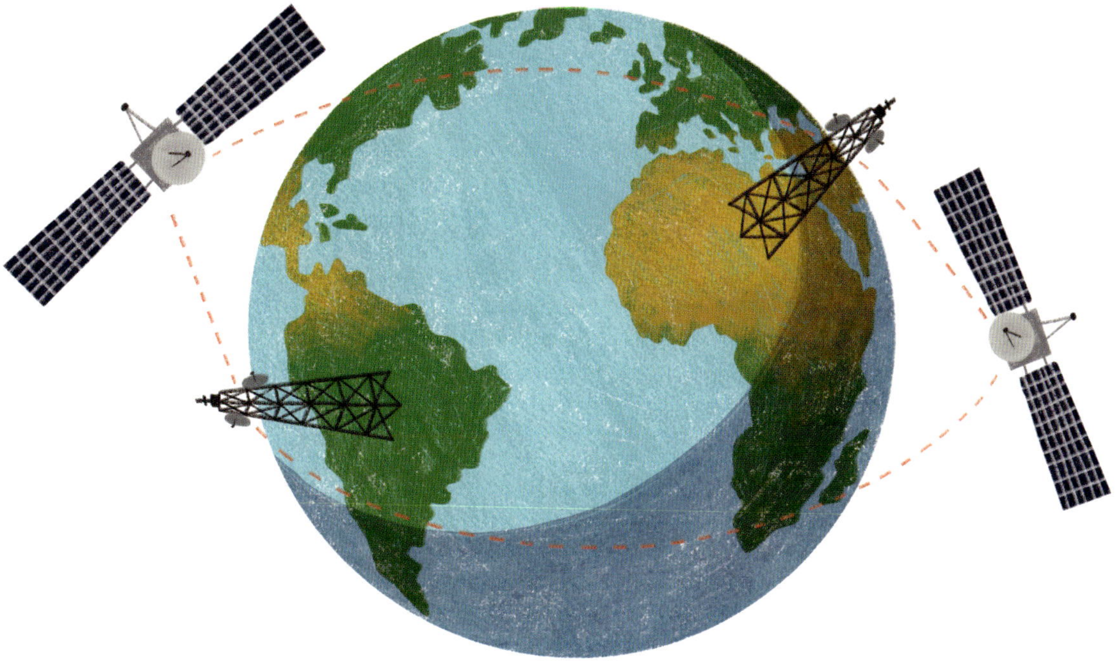

Computers can be connected in different ways. Some are linked by cables underground. Some use radio waves or connect to satellites—this is called a wireless connection.

Computers use the Internet to access websites. People can find information, do their shopping, and play games on websites.

WHAT MAKES A CAR MOVE?

Inside every car is an engine, which makes the car go.

Some cars use liquid fuel to power the engine. Burning the fuel moves parts called pistons up and down. Their movement is used to turn the wheels.

Some cars are powered by electricity, which is stored in a battery. Electric cars need to be plugged in to "charging points" to charge the battery.

As the pistons move up and down, they turn a part called the crankshaft.

The engine contains a row of pistons.

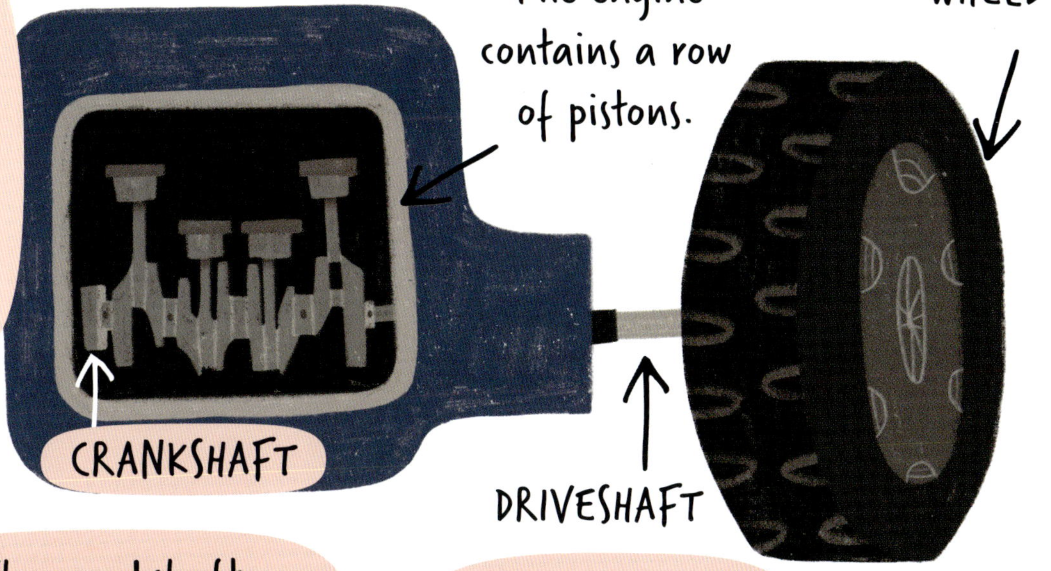

The crankshaft connects to a part called the driveshaft.

The driveshaft turns the wheels around, so that the car moves forward.

HOW DOES A MICROWAVE OVEN COOK FOOD?

If you want a quick, hot meal, put it in the microwave ... it will be ready in minutes!

Regular ovens cook by heating up the air around the food. In a microwave oven, food is cooked from the inside out.

Microwave ovens cook your food much quicker than ordinary ovens.

Inside a microwave oven is a magnetron. This sends out waves of energy called microwaves.

Microwaves make particles (very tiny parts) of water inside the food move quickly. This cooks the food.

A spinning fan bounces the microwaves around the inside of the oven and into the food.

HOW DOES A PIANO PLAY A TUNE?

A piano is a musical instrument with many strings inside. When you press a key, it makes the strings vibrate.

A guitar player plucks or strums the strings to create the sounds.

We hear sounds when an object vibrates, or makes small movements back and forth quickly. Musical instruments work by making vibrations in the air in different ways.

A piano can have around 230 strings. They are different lengths and thicknesses.

Short strings make high notes, and long strings make low notes.

When a piano key is pressed, a lever pushes a tiny hammer inside.

The hammer hits a string, which vibrates, making a sound. When the key is let go, a part called the damper moves down to stop the sound.

WHAT MAKES A TOILET FLUSH?

When you pull the flush handle, parts inside a toilet work together to take away dirty water and replace it with clean water.

The toilet cistern, or tank, is filled with clean water.

Parts called valves let water into the cistern. They also stop the water when it is full.

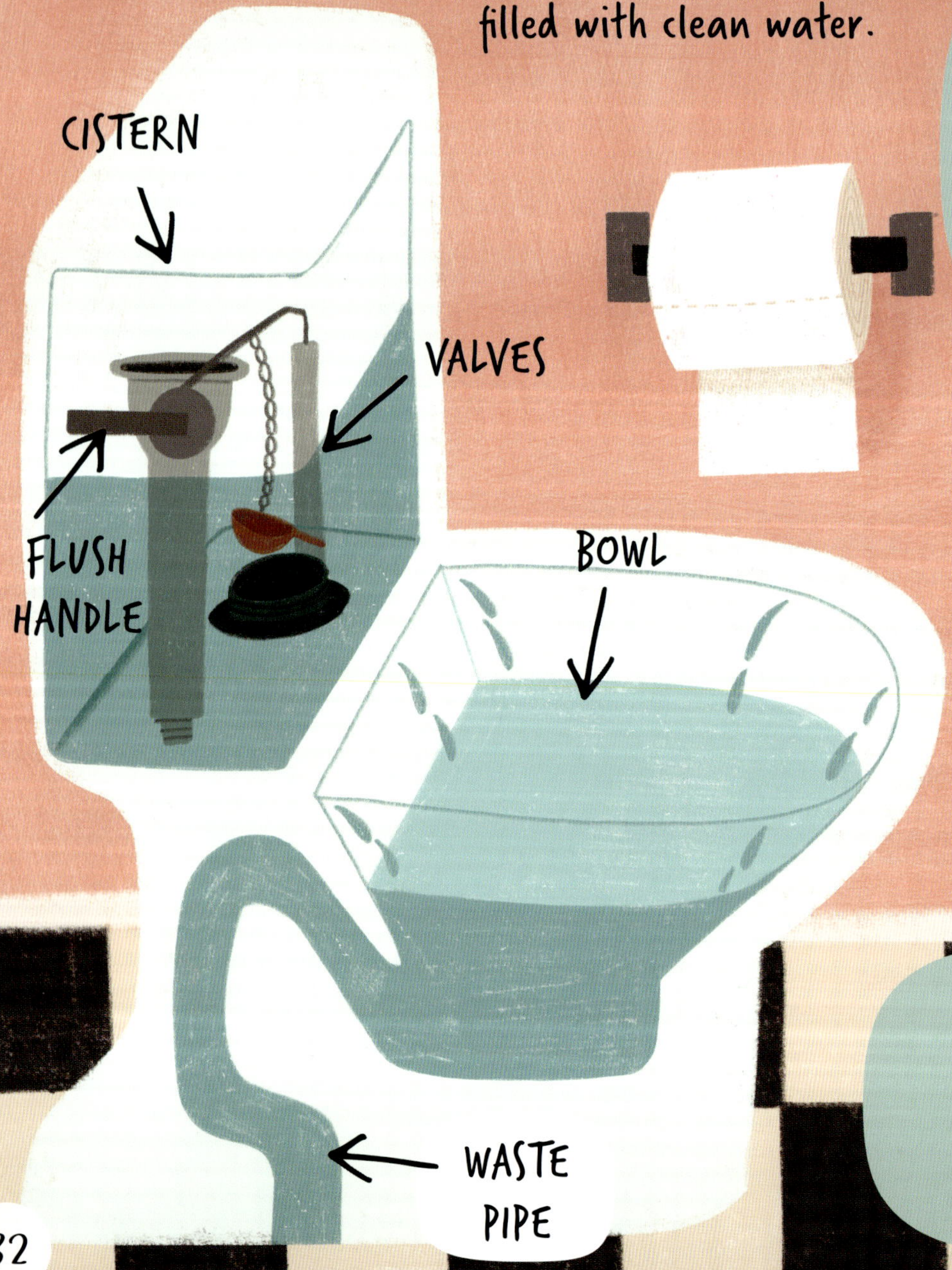

When you flush, the cistern opens and water travels into the toilet bowl.

The clean water pushes the dirty waste water out through the waste pipe.

Clean water is pumped through large pipes underground. Water flows through smaller pipes into our homes.

Waste (dirty) water flows out through different pipes into drains. It goes to "sewage treatment plants" to be cleaned and used again.

HOW DO TRAINS STAY ON THE TRACKS?

Trains can be powered by steam, electricity, or diesel fuel. But all types of trains travel along tracks.

Most trains travel along two rails. The rails are made of steel, which is a very strong metal.

The wheels on each side of a train car are attached to a metal rod called an axle.

The axle keeps the wheels moving together and turning at the same speed.

Each wheel has a rim called a flange. The flanges are slotted on the inside of the rail, which keeps them from moving outward and coming off the rail.

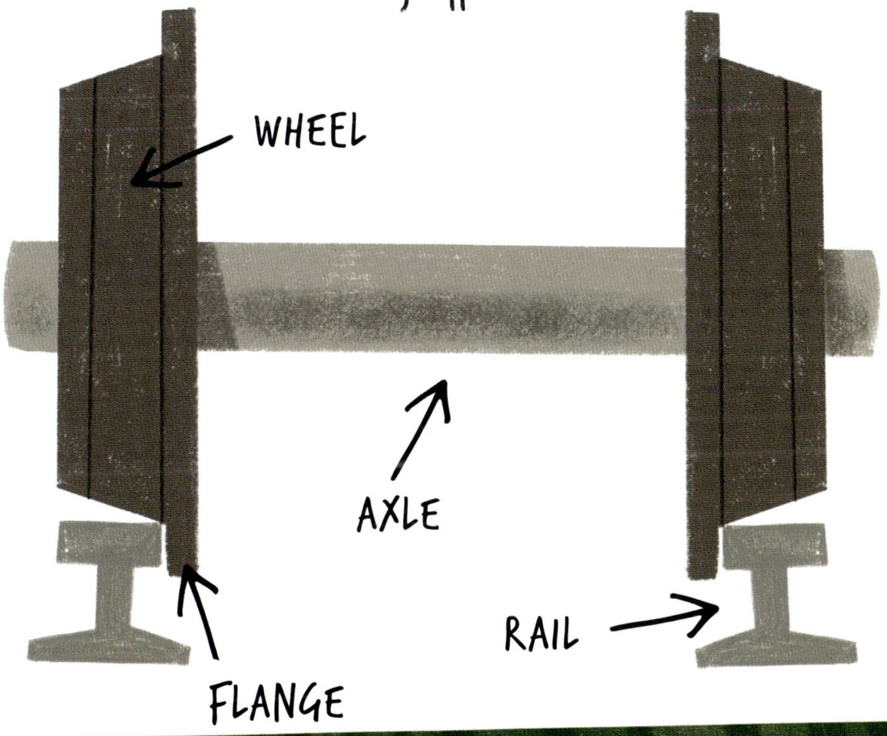

WHAT MAKES A HOT-AIR BALLOON GO UP?

Hot-air balloons are a beautiful sight, but how do they work?

Instead of an engine, a hot-air balloon uses something called a burner to make it fly.

When the pilot turns on the burner, it heats up the air inside the balloon. Hot air is lighter than the cold air outside, so the balloon floats up.

To go down, the pilot pulls a cord that opens a flap at the top of the balloon. This lets out some hot air, which makes the balloon go down.

Balloons can be different shapes and sizes.

The rounded balloon part, called the "envelope," is made of tough fabric. It is filled with air.

There is a basket underneath that carries the pilot and passengers.

HOW DOES A HAIRDRYER DRY MY HAIR?

Hairdryers blow out hot air to dry your wet hair in minutes.

Hairdryers need electricity to work.

When a hairdryer is switched on, electricity flows to a small motor inside.

The motor makes a fan spin really fast.

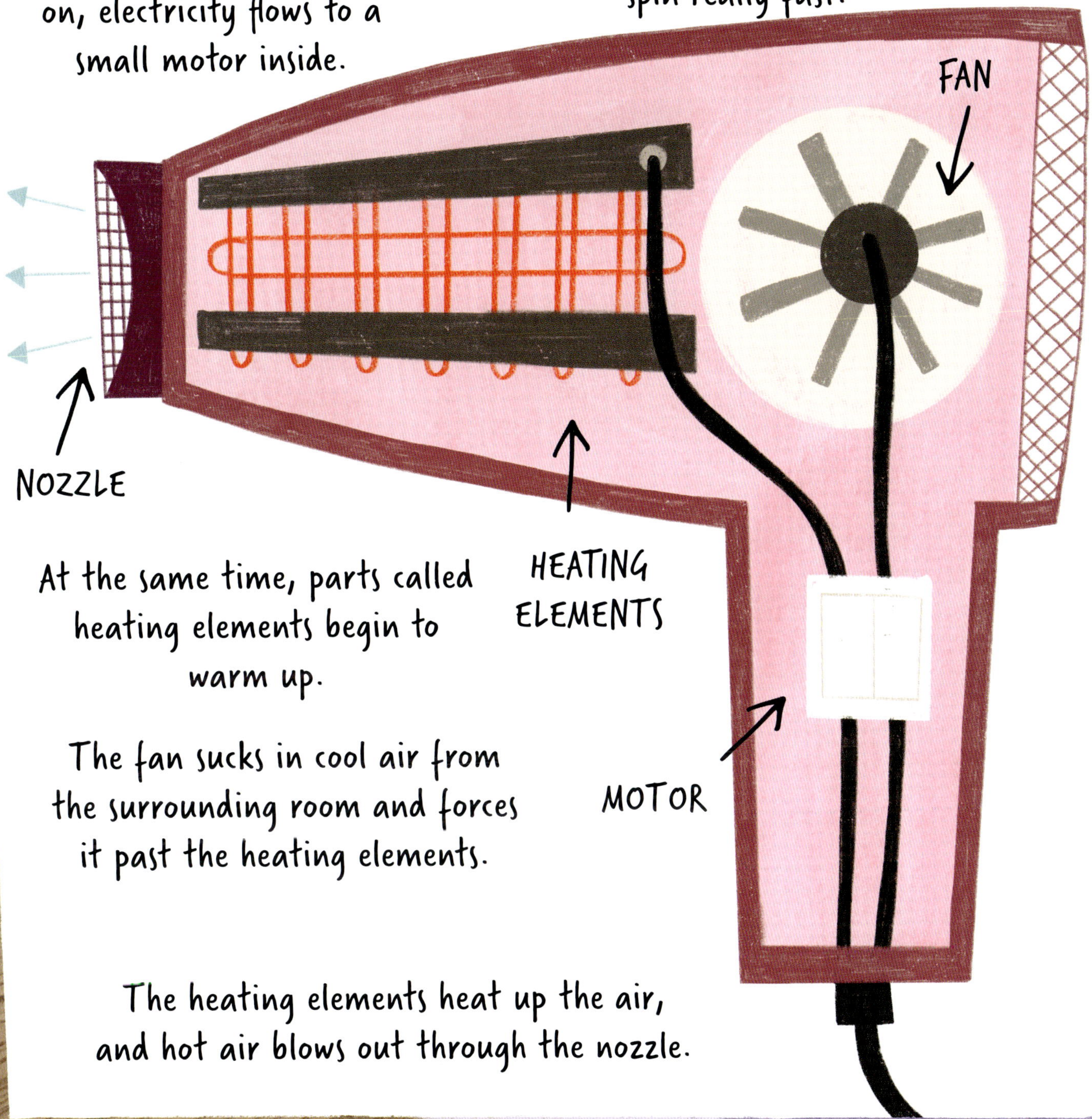

At the same time, parts called heating elements begin to warm up.

The fan sucks in cool air from the surrounding room and forces it past the heating elements.

The heating elements heat up the air, and hot air blows out through the nozzle.

HOW DO REFRIGERATORS KEEP FOOD FRESH?

Refrigerators work by warming and cooling something called a "refrigerant."

The refrigerant travels through pipes. The pipes run through the inside and outside of the refrigerator.

A part called the "expansion valve" changes the refrigerant from a liquid into a gas.

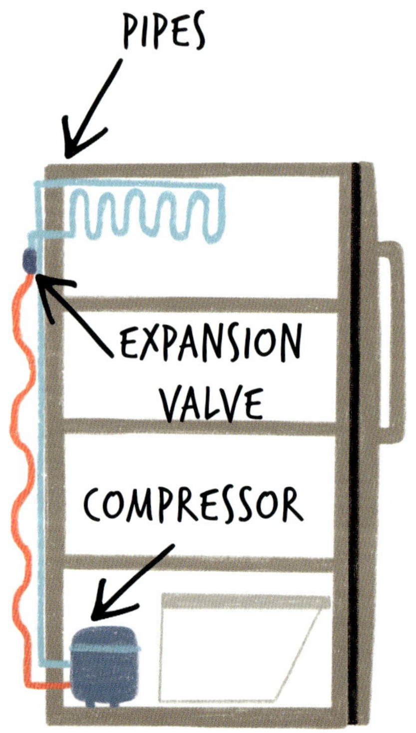

As it changes, the refrigerant takes away the heat from the inside of the refrigerator. This makes the refrigerator cooler.

As the gas leaves the inside part of the refrigerator, it flows through a type of pump called a "compressor."

The compressor squeezes the refrigerant, turning it back into a liquid. The heat is released through the pipes at the back and into the air.

The refrigerant flows back up to the expansion valve, ready to start all over again.

WHAT MAKES A CLOCK TiCK?

Clocks are machines that tell us what time of day it is.

A traditional mechanical clock has a face, where the numbers are. The hands show the hours and minutes.

Inside mechanical clocks, weights and cogs work together to move the hands.

Mechanical clocks need to be wound up regularly. When we wind up a clock, energy is stored in a weight.

Special toothed wheels, called cogs, move the energy around the parts, causing the hands to turn.

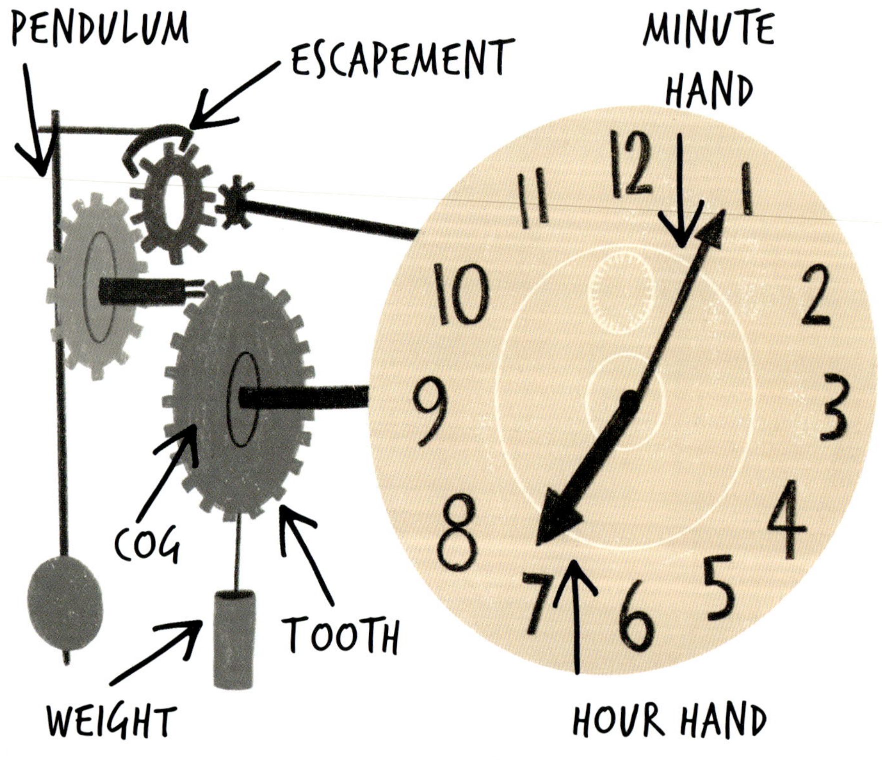

The escapement allows the cogs to turn, one tooth at a time. As each tooth moves through the escapement, it creates a ticking sound.

The pendulum is a swinging weight that controls how fast the teeth pass through the escapement.

Clocks can be mechanical or electrical.

Electrical clocks are powered by electricity. They often use batteries.

QUIZ: TRUE OR FALSE?

1

Bicycle pedals are connected to a gear.

2

Some shoes stay fastened with hook-and-loop fasteners.

3

Dishwashers need electricity and water to work.

4

Radio waves are invisible waves of energy that can travel through the air and space.

5

Helicopters can only fly forward and backward.

6

A computer processor acts like a brain.

QUIZ CONTINUED

7

In a microwave oven, food is cooked from the outside in.

8

Musical instruments work by making vibrations in the air in different ways.

9

A hot-air balloon uses a burner to make it fly.

10

Hairdryers need water to work.

11

The pipes in a refrigerator contain a special liquid called a "refrigerant."

12

Mechanical clocks do not need to be wound up.

ANSWERS:

1 True. 2 True. 3 True. 4 True. 5 False—helicopters can also fly up, down, and sideways! 6 True. 7 False—it is cooked from the inside out. 8 True. 9 True. 10 False—hairdryers need electricity to work. 11 True. 12 False—mechanical clocks need to be wound up regularly.

GLOSSARY

BATTERY A means of storing electricity.

COG A type of wheel with "teeth" around the outside edge. Cogs connect to and move other parts.

ELECTRICITY A type of energy. Machines that plug into sockets or have batteries use electricity.

ENERGY The power to do things.

FUEL A substance, such as petrol or diesel, that is burned in order to make energy.

GAS A substance that is not a solid or a liquid. A gas spreads out and has no fixed shape.

GEAR A wheel with "teeth" that connects to and turns another wheel. Gears are used to change the speed of something.

MICROPHONE A device that picks up sounds and turns them into electrical energy.

MICROWAVE A wave of energy that is able to pass through food and heat it up.

MOTOR A machine that is used to provide energy in order to move something.

NETWORK A group of things that are connected together, such as a computer network or a cellular phone network.

OXYGEN A natural gas in the air, that all living things need to survive.

RADIO WAVE An invisible wave of energy that can travel through the air and space.

VALVE An object that controls the flow of a gas or liquid.